Harvest the Day

Prose Poems by Margot Bickel
Photographs by Hermann Steigert

Edited by Gerhard E. Frost

11-14-85
To Margie
with every good
wish
Gerhard Frost

Winston Press

Designer: Nancy Condon
Translator: Katharine Fournier

Originally published in West Germany
under the title *Pflücke den Tag*
copyright © 1981 Verlag Herder Freiburg im Breisgau.

English-language edition
copyright © 1984 by Winston Press.
All rights reserved.
Printed in the United States of America.

5 4 3 2 1

ISBN: 0-86683-730-2

Winston Press
430 Oak Grove St.
Minneapolis, MN 55403

The birthing of a child
is like the early bud
of a flower
we watch with joy
and a tinge of sadness
as the unique one
makes every day its own
as if it were the first
and last

Those who leave room for others
who can laugh at themselves
such friends can really
laugh and cry with us

Long have we waited
to speak the reconciling word
to extend the trusting touch

Let's begin finally
to retrieve all that we've missed
in friendship

We've wasted ourselves in enmity
and no one knows what time is left
to make it up again

Come
take my hand

Harvest the day
for it is yours
to handle with care

Twenty-four hours
just time enough to give it worth
don't let it wither
in these early morning hours

Baking bread
breaking bread
sharing bread
being bread

It is too simple
to pet a stray dog
then watch it run under a car
and say it wasn't mine

It is too simple
to admire a rose
then pick it and forget
to put water in the vase

It is too simple
to use a person
for loving without love
then leave him standing alone
and say I don't know him
anymore

It is too simple
to know one's flaws
then live them at great cost to others
and say that's just the way I am

It is too simple
the way we sometimes live our lives
for after all life simply is
a serious matter

The older the tree
    the more its value and size
the deeper its roots
    the more steadfast its strength in the storm
the denser its branches
    the more certain its power to protect
the stronger its trunk
    the greater its support for the weary
the higher its crown
    the more inviting its shading umbrella

Each year-ring
a clear symbol
of lived strength
like a fold
in a face

A little peace
in the final hours
of the ebbing day
a little rest
between the days
to remember yesterday's becoming
and live tomorrow into today

Life and waves have this in common
they carry some things in
   and flush some things away
and with the coming of the tide
the waves flush the sandcastles
but push in a piece of wood
so the humble man
may fix the roof
of his hut

As birds rise majestically
cut circles as they spread their wings
and glide away
so we would rise
gain distance
and find our ways
exploring them in peace

As birds must land again
tuck in their wings
crouch on the ground
and seek their food
amid their many enemies
so we return to face this life
its dangers and demands

Sometimes I wish
I could be a boat for you
a boat to carry you
wherever you long to be
one that is sturdy and strong enough
for all the burdens you carry with you
and never capsizes
no matter how restless you are
or how stormy the sea
upon which we sail

Before my last breath is drawn
and the curtain falls
and the last flower falls on me
I want to live
   to love
   to be

In this gray world
and time of catastrophe
this hostile existence
with people who need me
and whom I need
I would learn to value
   to discover
   to be astonished

I want to learn who I am
   who I can be
   who I would like to be
so that the days don't go unused
the hours have goals
and the minutes value

Whenever I laugh or cry
or am silent
on my journey to you
   to myself
   to God
where the ways
   are uneven and thorny
and scarcely known to me
I want to set out
have already embarked
and don't want to turn back now
without having seen
   the blooming of flowers
or heard the rippling of waters
having been amazed
for life is beautiful

Then Friend Death may come
and I can say I have lived

Vulnerable to
life itself
to storms
and new captivities

I receive courage
joy and trust
and new liberations

On my journey from yesterday to tomorrow
I stretch out in the shadow of a tree
for a moment and think
about the road
where it leads
and of the way already traveled

I contemplate the blooming by the wayside
the fragrance that may never be stolen or abused
but only loved and cherished
in the joy of remembered things

I am aware
of the cold war within us
but feel more strongly still
the love we hunger for

I see the enmity and horror
of stubborn opposition
but sense in every struggle
the deeper wish to be together

I too am caught with you
in the fight for naked survival
but I surmise that we humans
at last suspect how high the stakes are

Our fascination with life
in spite of our knowing
that it is transient
may be founded on
the hazard of you
the courage of me
the wantonness of joy
upon our sense of humor
our exuberance of laughter
and our strength to survive our suffering

November fog
impenetrable
phantomlike
in my head
in my soul

My thoughts come to rest
my ideas remain opaque
my intentions unclear
yet my senses yield to refreshing sleep
anticipating the moment and the view
when the fog has withdrawn

November fog
in my head
in my soul

Only in that unreserved openness
and liberating emptiness
remaining after this stale earth
of principles and prejudices
has been pushed aside
is there hidden room
for new life and a new spirit

I can hold another's hand
another holds my hand
and my life

Caught bewitched and held
by the magic of living
seeing hearing touching smelling tasting
with eyes ears hands noses tongues
in order to experience
how life is and can be
caught bewitched and held

Sometimes I long
to be rays of sun for you
rays to warm your hands and dry your tears
to tickle your nose and make you laugh
rays of sun to lighten dark places
in your hidden person
and flood your routine
in brightest light
to melt the icebergs within you

The last rays at sunset
show the path
I would gladly take

The wind-driven clouds
show me the way
I would gladly go

The rustling leaves under my feet say
let yourself fall
and you will be free

Life's true gifts
are usually bestowed in stillness
friendship and love
birth and death
joy and pain
flowers sunrises silences
the larger dimensions
of human experience

Frozen
in the promise of spring
by icy rejection
loveless speech
and cold touch

Frozen
in midsummer
by sterile habit
disinterest
and cruel indifference

Frozen
in the ripeness of autumn
by contempt
mistrust
and hopeless condemnation

But melting
in icy midwinter
in the welcoming hand
the loving glance
and warm breath of life

At last even the realists
begin to dream of another life
the changed life in which they would begin anew
they dream as if it were reality
that steady drip which hollows stones

In awareness of such dreams
the realists apply themselves to what they see
happy to be able
to dream again

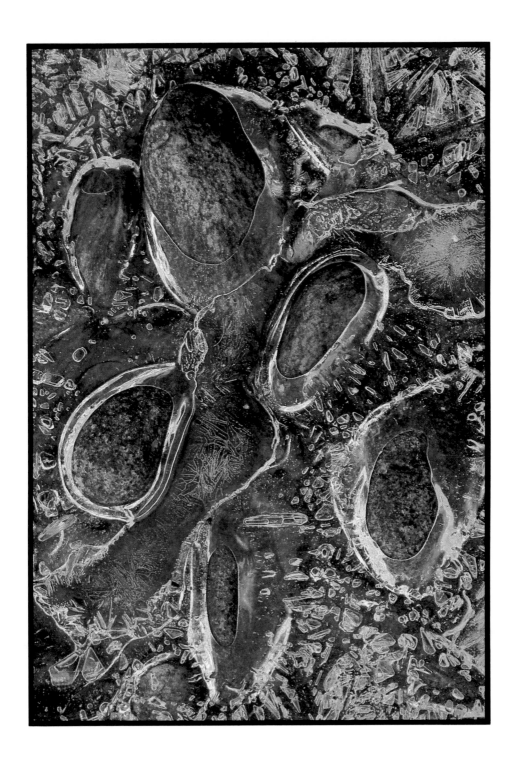

Perhaps we should renounce as superstition
our need to understand
and be reborn with the insight
that at best we may be able
to deal understandingly
with our lack of understanding

Our homeland is not in any place
however large the map may be
but only in the hearts
of those who love us

The day is coming
when water will flow upriver
snowflakes will stop in midair
children will ripen into grownups
and grownups into children
then the world will reverse its turning
the soil will whirl in eddies
and be fertile for reflection

Should someone then sow life again
humanity could reach full bloom
once more

Snow-blown hills
snow-blown trees
snow-blown paths
whoever trudges through the snow
leaves deep deep tracks
inviting us to follow
snow-filled hills
snow-filled trees
snow-filled paths
and always somewhere
tracks of living things

Do not fear
that the burden on your shoulders
will be more than you can bear
do not think you are too weak to carry it
and the burden of others

You will be amazed
at your power
at how strong you are
in spite of all your weakness

Reviews of the German edition:

"In a fascinating, continually engaging manner, the prose poems of Margot Bickel harmonize and expand the masterful photographs of Hermann Steigert. Each photo provides an aid to better understanding of the deeply thoughtful poems that deal primarily with the theme of life. This book will soon find a permanent place on the bookshelf of each friend of poetry and photography."
—*Schweize Jugend*

"This meditation book can inspire us to look deep and to find ourselves in nature. A gift worth recommending."
—*Mission Today*

"Shows in beautiful pictures how rich nature and life can be if you understand how to see, hear, and touch. . . . An impressive book for yourself or as a gift."
—*Nordbayerischer Kurier*

"Hermann Steigert's photos are the expression of a sensitive encounter, of finding one's self in nature. . . . This picture book for adults, which initiates meditation about one's self, is also appropriate as a gift. . . ."
—*Katholischer Kirchen-Anzeiger*, Rosenheim

"The new picture book *Pflücke den Tag [Harvest the Day]* from Herder Publishing is intended for quiet hours and meditation. . . . In a unique way, words about life, love, community, happiness, peace, and people's longing are combined with impressive photos of nature. . . . A book that is greatly to be recommended. . . ."
—*Bund der deutschen katholischen Jugend*

"What life is and can be is brought close to the reader and viewer of this excellent picture book. Rays of the sun breaking through the foliage, the tender leaf of a rose, the power of an ocean sunset, a spider's web, snow-covered hills and paths: wherever you open the book, the eye is renewed and inspired to read with all the senses."
—*Basis*